THE
UNCOVERED
GENIUS

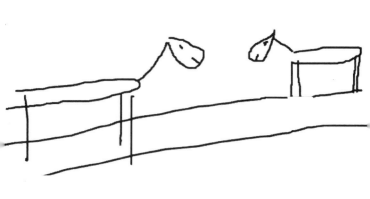

IVAN F. BALAKIREV

Edited by David W. Gao and Martin F. Naud

Published by DEJ
ISBN 978-1-387-82762-6

CONTENTS

To my editors and my dreamers

FOREWORD

For the past four years, I have had the distinct pleasure of interacting with Mr. Balakirev in the ritual known as high school. His mind has proven to be a vast expanse of unique knowledge and insight. Ivan possesses a passion for truth, one that cannot be expressed through conventional writing and tradition. Accordingly, this work has been completed primarily through voice-typing, having been edited into English Vernacular for widespread distribution (through the work of Martin Naud and myself). The raw, unedited version of this work is also available.

This book represents but a glimpse of Mr. Balakirev's philosophies and revelations. It is a book of many concepts: ice hockey, god, vitamins. It intertwines the varied and rich experiences of the author's life with statistics, science, and philosophy. It is a book of truth.

David Gao
Undergraduate at UCLA

VITAMINS ARE USELESS

Vitamins—people take them and feel better about themselves for it. People take multivitamins and other types of vitamins so that they can supposedly reach their vitamins cap and have a healthier body. While on the surface this may seem true, in practice the body does not actually use any of this micronutrient for anything other than creating very expensive urine.   Micronutrients such as the vitamin C and the vitamin B complex are water soluble. This means that these two vitamins can be dissolved in water; that is why you see many vitamin supplements such as Emergen-C and other things have more than your percentage value for your average 2000 calorie day. The packets claim to provide 240% of your daily caloric needs for different vitamins. This means that about almost all the vitamin C or B that you're drinking and eating is waste product and your body doesn't need it. So you pee it out, and guess what, those packets aren't cheap kids, they're pretty expensive...one box can run you 15 bucks and next thing you know your pee is worth 15 bucks. Who wants 15 bucks in their pee? No one no one wants that. Now you may be asking about all the other vitamins saying "I remember A through K in my elementary school huh what about them?" Well, these vitamins are fat soluble, so if you eat too much your body stores it in fat. This could be a problem 'cuz if you eat way too much you may become sick from over-nutrification as I like to call it. Your body won't be able to do its tasks as usual because it has too many vitamins. Now you may say "I can store these vitamins so that means I can actually still buy these over the counter." Yeah sure, you can buy over the counter — pay your $30 for all of your pill packets. However, you can get all of these vitamins that you'll need for your average life from fresh fruits and veg. Those are like $0.50 a pop and boom! All your vitamin needs are there, you don't need to take vitamin supplements. They're lies, they're just companies preying on dumb consumers, hoping that they say "I need more vitamins in my life. I should probably take supplements to help me lift you know." And for other vitamins such as Vitamin D, because your body makes them yourself, just go outside sometimes — put on sunscreen so you don't get melanoma, easy peasy. The only times you'll ever need to take vitamins are: if your doctor says so — since you're diseased — or if you're malnourished from deciding to only eat potatoes for the rest of your life. Don't be dumb — just eat fruits and veg, you'll be good.

The only thing that a person should make sure they do more of is to drink water. Drinking at least a liter an hour or just making sure you drink water helps lubricate your bones. You may say "I don't want to get fat from water." Bloating only happens if you don't drink water for a long time, because your body will retain that water as it thinks that it won't get any more water. If you're dehydrated you'll be dead because you're 70% water; ergo, you need the water. If you just keep drinking, you'll lose that water to an extent because your body just decides *I don't need this water, I just need dreams* and expels water through the urethra. One time, I was sick and for a week all I drank was water and I lost 10 lb. This wasn't from sickness; I lost water weight because all I did was drink water, so I became actually hydrated. When you do this in real life, make sure you food, or else you can have a bad day. Because I was not moving all day, I didn't need food, but average people walk, so they need food. So just drink water, make sure you drink lots and lots and lots of water.

You also want water because water helps the body accomplish biological tasks such as reactions between cells. You need vitamins for this, but you also need water. So make sure you stay out of Vitamin City and only go to Hydration City. Talking about vitamins leads me to my next chapter...I'm talking about drinks. When you find a drink, make sure it does not promise any health benefits, as that is a load of lies.

KOMBUCHA, KOMBUCHA

Health drinks — the people that talk about them say they're the next best thing. "I drink health drinks all my life, I am a god now." No, they don't work like that, they're all fake. Look at Vitamin Water: nothing but sugar and water, ain't no vitamins in that. Someone even tried to sue Vitamin Water for not being healthy. However, Vitamin Water retorted "no consumer could reasonably be misled into thinking vitaminwater was a healthy beverage." In the 21st century a new drink has hit the block, and it's popular. Kombucha. People are going nuts over it and say it is the piss of Jesus, that after taking it they fly to a new life literally and figuratively — new kombucha, new me. What's this? It's fake facts, that's what it is. Kombucha, for those that don't know the prophecy, is a fermented tea drink. You ferment that, a month or two later, kombucha is born. Depending on who you ask it's either the best thing since Jesus or it's a dumpster. From my tone of voice in this piece you may assume I hate kombucha; I don't, I just dislike it's cult following. It's no health drink, there's no super tricks, kombucha is just a drink and that's all it is. Whether you love it or hate it, it's just a drink. You drink Pepsi, I drink tea, and it doesn't matter. They're both drinks. But did Pepsi or tea say that Jesus will fix all your problems? Running late to work— drink kombucha— have divorce—drink kombucha—dog diet— drink kombucha—Laura is in hospice— Kombucha, kombucha, kombucha. Just like Pepsi Pepsi. They're just drinks, they taste good to some and other people would rather have Cola. Don't drink too much Pepsi and don't drink too much kombucha or else you will have a bad time. They just want to take your money; go drink a glass of water, it's better for you. People have died from making their own kombucha because they mess up the fermentation process...boom whoopsie doopsie they dead. So if you're going to partake in the Kombucha

Revolution, you'll want to just buy it yourself because you will probably kill yourself (you're dumb, you're reading this book). If in the next 10 to 20 years, a new health drink comes out that tells you will fix your life, your wife will come back, your dog resuscitated itself, Laura survives hospice, and you somehow appear to work on time, no it won't happen—go drink some water. The only time when you're going to drink some health drinks is when your doctor says you're going to drink that. And usually that drink tastes terrible—tastes like my uncle Vinny on a hot summer morning. Stick to water, you don't want Uncle Vinny in your mouth.

PAIN IS FALSE

"Untrue!" you say. "You feel pain all the time!"

I'm not talking about emotional or actual physical pain; real pain is caused by real problems. I'm talking about pain that your mind makes up. It's called *pepper pain*. Whenever you eat hot foods, you feel pain on your tongue. This is false pain. Think of the Norse god Loki, dancing on your tongue, making up pain so that you do not eat the food that you eat. The reason that this pain is false is that it's created by the plant that you eat, using a chemical called capsaicin. As you eat the capsaicin, receptors on your tongue send chemical signals through neurons to your brain, telling your mind that you are in pain. One way to stop this false pain is to get something to bind to the capsaicin, so that the capsaicin doesn't bind to your tongue receptors. Some methods to stop the pain is to drink milk as milk will bind to capsaicin however this is not a foolproof method if you want complete pain relief making a cocktail out of soap and shampoo will eliminate most of the capsaicin in your mouth. This is why water does not stop the burning sensation and actually spreads the heat throughout your mouth water does not bind to capsaicin, water just moves capsaicin around your mouth so the capsaicin can find more of your receptors, so you feel more pain. However, because this pain isn't real and it's just plants making you *think* you have pain, the mind can overcome it if you take training exercises and believe there is no pain. Just like a monk's mind over matter, you become one with yourself and feel zero pain.

ROADS ARE IMPOSSIBLE

In recent pop culture, there are many shows in the high middle ages or shows that take fantasy elements from the middle ages. One thing these shows get wrong every single time is how roads work. The roads on the shows have two lines that go on for endless miles and that is how roads work for cars—they have two wheels on each side, they move down the road, and there's lines on each side. However, a horse carriage differs in that it is not moved by an engine but by a horse. For a horse to move a carriage, it has to be either in the middle of the carriage or on a side. And when a horse trots on the ground so frequently, these footpaths would not have two sides to them, but would be completely effaced in the middle as this is where the beast of burden would move most often. Critics may say "Well, the road is fertilized from horse poop, so the grass grows back faster in the middle." However, if that was the case, the entire Road would grow back fast. Look at other movies where they actually use horses to move things; in those movies, horses and carriages create such a mess in the mud the grass isn't even visible. Additionally, if people rode solely on horseback, there would only be one lane instead of two. Horses can just go around each other, unlike carriages they don't have wheels and can sustain travel on rough ground. In the end, the correct horse path will just look like one gigantic lane. As different carriages and horses use the path, it'll all eventually just become dirt and no grass.

CAST IRON LIE

Not only have movies gotten roads wrong, but they also are wrong in their production of weapons—more specifically, swords and other bladed objects. In most movies, they show molten iron being poured into a mold (in even more egregious acts, into half a mold). This can be seen in *The Lord of the Rings* as the Uruk-hai pours molten iron into half-molds to create their swords. Now, if you have a sword at home, you may say "oh, the manufacturer said they casted the sword—it's a real sword, ain't it?"

It's not. The cast sword in your house is a decoration. It is not built for combat and it cannot withstand combat; so whenever you join a crusade, do not take the decorative sword that hangs on your wall. Think of melting iron; once you melt the iron, it acts like a pool of ping pong balls. Now, you take these ping pong balls and pour them into a mold; then, all the metal does is cool down when it chills in the mold. Eventually, it cools enough for it to become rock hard, or should I say metal hard hehe. However when you look at the ping-pong-structure of this cast metal, it isn't an organized lattice of ping pong balls. Since the iron is unevenly cooled and weighed down by "gravity," air bubbles become trapped in the ping pong pool. If you were to slice this cast iron object, you would see that there are tiny holes everywhere. For an expendable metal object, like a cannonball, this does not matter because big whoop your cannonball booped. However, if a person is trying to make a sword—a nice thin slice of metal used to cut someone with—cast iron will show its faults, the air bubbles greatly compromise the sword's strength. A sword or other weapon used for slicing or hacking should be able to withstand repeated abuse, and be able to block or parry a sword or other hacking device. If a sword is too brittle, it will shatter and rendered useless. So, to cast is a ghast blast leading to a fast dismast, and should be lambaste.

This is why if you go to a traditional smithy, you see a blacksmith hammering away at hot iron bars. Hammered iron is called wrought iron. This means that all the little bubbles that are forming in the iron are smashed into each other. If you were to cut open a wrought iron piece, you would find that it looks like string cheese — it has many, many, many tiny layers. Also, you can tell if iron has been wrought and properly cooled if the iron is no longer magnetic. There is some evidence that weapons were casted during the Bronze Age; as described, they are very brittle. Since most of the casting of the metal went to the blade, the handle had to be riveted and was too, very weak. Lo and behold, Bronze Age swords broke quickly. Another reason why molds are not used, is the mold itself is very easy to break. Because the mold is made out of rock, it is vulnerable to thermal shock when heated too quickly. Movies, if they're using a mold, often don't even use a correct mold. Going back to the Uruk-hai from *The Lord of the Rings*, the blades they made were poured into an open mold and only half the mold was there. This does not make any sense, as only half the iron would be in the shape of a sword, while the other half would be unformed. As the iron cools, all the outgassing will have the air-exposed side become littered with craters and susceptible to rusting. As you would expect, the sword would be useless. All steel items that must sustain repeated impacts must be repeatedly impacted.

RATS ARE REAL

Have you ever seen a giant rat in a video game and say to yourself, "that's just a fantasy." Well, turns out those rats are kind of possible. To discuss the subject, one must first learn about cells — most importantly, the haploid and diploid cells that go through meiosis. Now, human cells that go through meiosis are located in the testes, and these cells are called sperm. Each sperm is a haploid cell with the genetic information needed to create life. The other haploid cell that the sperm needs to combine with to form life is the egg. Located inside a human female, this egg is also haploid and also has about half the genetic information needed for life. When two haploids meet they will combine into a diploid zygote. This cell is totipotent and can divide, eventually becoming a human fetus. However, if more than one sperm enters the egg, the cell can become a triploid or greater. Now the problem with a triploid is that it's not viable for life, because the sperm DNA cannot make homologous pairs with other chromosomes as there's just not the right number of chromosomes to form homologous pairs. This is why when only an even amount of haploids combine can they then form homologous pairs. So for a polypoid animal that has, say, three sperm enter an egg, it will be able to form homologous pairs because there is an even amount of haploids. In humans, having a polyploid fetus will end in stillbirth because humans are unable to support this type of life…however, the creation of a viable polyploid fetus has been recorded and seen in animals such as rats. It has been noticed that the polyploid fetus will be bigger than most other fetuses. So here's my theory: instead of one sperm entering an egg, how about 5001 entering the egg? The rat that is born will be huge and grotesque. This fantasy—a massive, super aggressive, and very strange looking rat—is reality.

THE UNIVERSE AND IT'S BIG BOYOS

SECTION I

      "So what is the universe?" you ask. Well, it's God. What is God? God is the ruler of the universe and all its magical mysteriousness. Some people say what I say God is—the ruler of our physical world and *only* our world. A distinction I must make before moving on: one must realize that there are multiple gods, and "God" is only the god of our world, Earth, and he controls everything on it—well, everything that he can see. You may feel a pressure on yourself that is roughly 9.8 meters per second squared down on you, this is the power of God's gaze. Scientists may say this is gravity; however, Believers know this is God's gaze. When God looks at something, the pressure of his gaze launches itself onto the receiver and the receiver feels this gaze as pressure, scientists quantify this as 9.8 meters per second squared. The principle of God's gaze explains many quandaries about our material world, like why space travel is so hard — once a rocket escapes our atmosphere, it will no longer under God's domain as it will be in the Eternal Darkness ruled by the Void Lords (don't worry, this is a topic discussed in a later section). Another modern quandary that God's gaze expels is quantum mechanics. When a scientist tells you that quantum mechanics is hard and very confusing — frankly, it makes no sense — it is because God cannot see the quantum world, it is too small for God to easily visibly see. This is why some principles of quantum mechanics work the way they do. For example, when observing a particle in quantum mechanics, it is impossible to know both the state of the particle — it could either be going left, right, spinning up or down — and its exact position. This "uncertainty principle" is because God cannot see this particle and cannot, himself, define both its position and momentum; ultimately, scientists, being inferior to God, also cannot observe them. The reason the uncertainty principle is uncertain is because God is uncertain and when God isn't certain we are not certain.

Some groups may say there is only one God. And other groups may say that the moon landing was faked...both these groups are wrong. The moon landing was indeed true; however, the science that brought them there was false. When an object leaves the sphere of influence about Earth, it leaves God's grounds and enters a realm that God cannot control, as he is too small of a being compared to other beings that have lived in the void for millennia. These beings that live in the void, called the Void Lords, have been ruling over this dark territory for millennia. They search for the Quantum Points (or as I like to call it, the new Big Bang). These Quantum Points carry a great amount of energy. And this energy is what the Void Lords use as their "food". You may look at a black hole and think "That is terrifying." However, that is the mouth of a Void Lord. So as a rocket ship leaves God's sphere of influence, it will no longer be bound by the same physics that was on Earth. This is why space travel is very hard, because scientists must not only account for God's gaze, but also the Void Lord's domain. The only reason scientists have reached the Moon is because they were able to discover the secrets of Void Lord Gilgamesh's domain; through this venture into his secrets, scientists are able to understand how his domain interacts with an object. Using this information, we are able to reach the minor Supreme Being called the Moon.

Also contrary to popular belief, the Moon comes from God. As God was once attacked in the ancient Wars of Ozmosis, God has lost its supposed gallbladder and this gallbladder orbits God's domain in the void. Supposedly, this explains the movements of the ocean. As God's bowels move back and forth, the water moves back and forth. When God is sick and his stomach hurts, something bad happens on Earth—such as an earthquake within the ocean (humans define this as natural disaster).

SECTION II

As believed by many scientists, the creation of the universe seems to be "The Big Bang". However, this is a misconception of what really happened. In the twilight of the universe, a "Big Bang" did occur; however, it did not create what we believe to be the elements that make up the universe now. The Big Bang created the Supreme Being. Now, this Supreme Being—being very bored— created the first Void Lords. These Void Lords rule over their voids with immense power and eventually created their own suns, which would be called galaxies. According to scripture, a group of Void

Lords, jealous of the Supreme Being's power, decided to rise up and fight the Supreme Being. After almost a million years of war, the Void Lords prevailed, leaving the universe a fiery mess. However, when they destroyed the Supreme Being, the Supreme Being exploded; this is why the universe is ever-expanding. The energy from the Supreme Being has permeated throughout the universe, creating minor beings such as our own God. The Void Lords of old have captured most of the energies and created their own domains. A Void Lord uses a black hole as its mouth for gathering energy. And because of a Void Lord's fierce eyes, it is able to control most of what it sees in its galaxies. This also explains heliocentricity — as the sun looks at its solar system, it controls each of its planets. However, Earth's God was able to stop most of our Sun's control with the magnetic field. Using this magnetic field, God is able to hide the fact that there are beings on Earth. That is why God makes space travel so hard; God doesn't want beings to escape the Earth and attract other Lords & beings who wish to eat God. Scientists have predicted that in about a billion years, the Sun will finally gain enough energy to be able to break through the magnetic field and finally see what's on Earth's crust—killing God in the process.

THE NHL TILTS

I would call myself a hockey fan. In my avid watching of this meticulous and beautiful sport, I've noticed something very peculiar. Every time a hockey match starts, the home team seems to have an advantage and controls the puck in the opposing side for most of the first period. During the second period the teams switch sides and so does the pace of the game. During the second period, the opposing team is now controlling the puck and is able to score goals during this second period. In the third period the teams switch sides again and a very obvious thing happens — the home team now gains overall possession of the puck and pace of the game. After pondering this quandary for a sizable chunk of my life, I have come to the only solution that can possibly explain this phenomenon: *the ice has been tilted*. Why would any other

35

explanation be false? Well, some say that a team will have a better strategy coming out the locker room. But this is false because hockey is lucky (kinda). It's also skill but it's also lucky, so coaching and strategy is negligible to the Supreme Theory. The only theory that can explain the strange phenomenon is that the ice is tilted. So the reason it's so hard for hockey players to stop and have equal possession is because it's hard to ice-skate uphill. I've done it, it's hard. Now a person may ask "Why does the NHL tilt their ice? That's unfair." You might say "No, it's not fair." But the reason they do this is because hockey is unpredictable, and nobody really scores unless they have an advantage. Now the tilt is not insignificant; from my calculations, the tilt is about 4 degrees. You may say "4 degrees? That's a small number" and I might say you're right. But when you're sprinting up a 4 degree incline, and it's icy, and you're sliding down the other way, it's pretty hard. Friction is hard. People may ask "How do you get a 4 degree tilt in your ice? When I fill my ice tubs back at home, I have flat ice." The tilted ice comes from the one and only Zamboni. It has a weird name so it means it's a weird thing. The Zamboni has a refrigerator on the bottom; when water molecules are placed on top of each other, they're frozen superfast. Think of taking a tablecloth off a table and leaving the glass on top just got to go really fast. Works the same for ice just put the water on and freeze it before it levels out. Do that over and over again until you have a 4 degree incline on your entire icy surface. Critics of this theory state that the Zamboni has only been recently invented...so how could have the 4 degree tilt be done in the olden days?

I must now speak of the Great Canadian Ice Carvers. Back in 1803, hockey was invented by the Jesuit Indians. In British Columbia, a problem was occurring. By 1850, nobody could score a goal. They tried, but they couldn't. Ice is slippery — it's kind of hard to go up and down when all you have are moccasins. So an ancient tradition was revitalized, and this was Ice Carving. Hockey players thought to themselves, "Well if I can't move on the ice, what if I make gravity move me on the ice?" And so back around 1917 when the first six NHL teams were formed, the Ice Carvers would show up before every game, and then meticulously carve a beautiful 4 degree angle with hammer and chisel. This was the great goal scoring era, as teams could not handle the incline advantage. However, after the advent of the ice skate, both teams could score even with the tilt.

UNEDITED VERSION

(For those who like to practice grammar)

Vitamins are useless

Vitamins people take them and feel better about themselves for it. People take multivitamins and other types of vitamins so that they can supposedly reach their vitamins cap and have a healthier body. while on the surface this may seem true and practice the body does not actually use any of this micronutrient for anything other than creating very expensive urine. micronutrients such As the as vitamin C and the B complex are water soluble. This means that these two vitamins can be dissolved in water thus drunk that is why you see many packet such as emergency and other things have more than your percentage value for your average 2000 calorie day. some say you are 240% of your daily caloric needs this means that about almost all the vitamin C or B that you're drinking and eating is as waste product and your body doesn't need it so your pee it out guess what those packets a cheap kids they're pretty expensive one box can run your 15 bucks and next thing you know your p is worth 15 bucks who wants 15 bucks in there p no one no one wants that. now you may Maybe asking about all the other vitamins saying I remember a through K in my elementary school huh what about them. well these vitamins are fat soluble so if you eat too much your body stores in fat this could be a problem cuz of you way too much you make you come sick from over Nutri fication as I like to call it so your body won't be able to do its tasks as usual because it's too many vitamins now you may sayI can store these vitamins so that means I can actually still buy these over the counter yeah sure you can buy over the counter pay your $30 for all of your pill packets however you can get all of these vitamins that you'll need for your average life fresh fruits and veg those are like $0.50 a pop and boom all your vitamin needs are there you don't need to take vitamin supplements their lies they're just companies preying on dumb consumers hoping that they say I need more vitamins in my life I should probably take supplements to help me lift you know. and for other vitamins such as Vitamin D cuz your body makes yourself so I just go outside sometimes you know so you don't get melanoma easy peasy. The only time you'll ever need to take vitamins if your doctor say sews that's only if you have a disease or are just malnourished and decided to eat only potatoes for the rest of your life so you're not getting any vitamins don't be dumb just eat fruits and veg you'll be good.

the only thing that a person should make sure they do more of is to drink water drinking at least delete an hour I think I may be less just make sure you drink water folks helps lubricate your bones and you may say I don't want to get fat from water only happens if you don't drink water for a long time cuz in your body retain that water because it it stinks and I can get water for like the next 2 days I may as well just taking this water and not expel it cuz if you're dehydrated the dead cuz you're just 70% water. if you just keep drinkingWhy you lose that water body late to an extent because your white your body just decides I don't need this water I just need dreams and sore expels water through urethra. one time I was sick and there are there for a week was drink waterI lost 10 lb this wasn't from sickness because I lost from water week cuz all I do is drink water and I was actually hydrated now when you do this in real life make sure you food or else you can have a bad day cuz I was moving all day so sick so I didn't need food but average people walk so they need food so just drink water make sure you drink lots of lots of lots of water.

You don't want it also helps your body to helps your body do body things such as reactions in your body between yourselves you need vitamins for this but you also need water so make sure you stay out of vitamin City and only go to hydration City. Talking about vitamins leads me to my next my next chapter I'm talking about drinks what do you think of a drink make sure don't have no health benefits cuz if it do the whole lot of cow manure.

Kombucha, it ain't good for ya but it ain't bad either

Super drinks people talk about him say the next best thing I drink super drinks all My life I am God now. no they don't work like that they all fake. look up vitamin water nothing but sugar and water ain't no vitamins in that. someone try to soon by Alan Wilder tell him to say healthy next plus we said this is not a health drink this is a sugary drink this is why I don't bother does not bring any help vetements that is bad for you. now in the 21st century a new drink has hit the black and it's Popular. look it's in the side of this piece kombucha people going nuts over it say it say Jesus is piss that after taking it they fly to the life literally and figuratively new me new kombucha who dis it's fake facts that's what it is. kombucha for those that don't know the prophecy is a fermented drink to take chia seeds to take tea and I ferment that s*** guess what a month later or a week later between that time span kombucha is born depends on who you ask it's either the best thing since Jesus or it's a dumpster. for my tone of voice in this piece you made assume I hate kombucha I don't I just dislike it's cold following it's no super drink there's no super tricks kombucha it's just a drink that's all it is whether you love it what do you hate it it's just a drink. you drink Pepsi I drink tea it doesn't matter that both drinks butDid all Pepsi or tea don't do say that Jesus will fix all your problems all running late to work drink kombucha have divorce drink kombuchaDog diet drink kombucha. call Laura hospice Kombucha kombucha like Pepsi Pepsi they just drink they taste good to some and other people rather have Cola. Don't drink too much Pepsi and don't drink too much kombucha in a bad time just want to take your money go drink a glass of water it's better for you. People eating tide for making their own kombucha cuz they mess up the fermentation process send whoopsie doopsie they Dead. So if you're going to partake in the kombucha Revolution probably just want to buy it yourself cuz you probably kill yourself cuz you're dumb you reading this book. if inthe next 10 to 20 years and new super drink comes out those you will fix your life your wife will come back your dog or resuscitated selfyou're somehow appeal to work on time no it won't happen go drink some water. the only time when you going to drink some super drink is when your doctor says you're going to drink that drink and usually that drink taste terrible taste like my uncle Vinny on a hot summer morning you don't want Uncle Vinny in your mouth stick to water.

Pain is false

untrue you say you feel pain all the time I'm not talking about emotional or actual physical pain I'm talking about paying your mind makes up. it's called pepper pain whenever you eat hot foods you feel pain on your tongue this isn't true pain this is false. think of the Norse god Loki dancing on your tongue making up pain so that you do not eat the food that you eat. the reason this pain is false is because it's created by the plant that you eat using a chemical called capsaicin as you eat the capsaicin Vines to your scepters on your tongue and sends chemical signals through neurons to your brain telling your mind that you are in pain. One way to stop this false pain is to get something to buy to these capsaicin so that it doesn't bind to your tongue receptors some say to drink milk other say to take a swig of soap. That is why when you drink water you You still feel pain because water does not bind to capsaicin it just moves it around your mouth so it can find some more of your receptors so you feel more pain. However, Because this pain is real and it's just plants making you think you have pain the mind can overcome it if you take training exercises and believe believe there is no pain just like monks a mind over matter you become one with yourself and feel zero pain.

Road's are Impossible

And recent pop culture there are
many shows in the high or shows that take
fantasy elements from the Middle Ages. one
thing these shows get wrong every single
time is how Rose work The roads are nice
shows have two lines that go on for Endless
miles and I'm you think that's how Rhodes
work but can you think of a car they have
four wheels two on each side they move
down the road and there's lines on each side
and then you think of a horse carriage it
has has four wheels two on each side and it
also makes lines down the road however
people often forget that in the Medieval ages
they didn't have engines but had Horses
and for a horse to move a carriage it has to
be either in the middle or onto on either side
and when a horse moves that walks on the
ground so often these footpaths would not
have two sides to them but would be
completely downtrodden in the exact
middle as where this is where the Beast of

Burden would move most often. critics may
say that well the grass in the Middle with
the old fertilized from horse poop so it grow
back fast however if that was the case then
the entire Road or grow back fast;. look at
other movies where they actually use horses
to move things and those movies horses and
carriages create such a mess in the mud the
dirt isn't even visible. Another Counterpoint
what do people instead of on characters just
rode on horseback however why would
there be two lanes instead of one.

Casting aint real

Movies have not also goten roads wrong but they have also gotten wrong how weapons are made. More specifically swardas and other bladed objects. In most movies it shows molten Iron being poured into a mold in even more egregious acts into half a mold. This can be seen in the lord of the rings as the urki poor molten iron into half molds to create their swords. now if you have a sword at home you may say all the manufacturer said they cast The Sword it's a real sword isn't it. it's not. the sword that is cast in your house is a decoration is not built for combat and cannot withstand combat so if you ever have a to go on a crusade do not take it here decorative sword that hangs on your wall. for the science of white casting a sword is bad. think melting iron it as you melt a brick it's a little marbles / ping pong balls now you take these ping pong balls and pour them all into a mold and all the metal does is cool down after it's in the mold eventually it's cool enough for it's rock hard or should I say metal hard heh. however when you look at the structural Integrity of this cast metal it is just a bunch of ping pong balls stuck together And because all Iron has to wait down is Gravity the cast iron objects will bubble. if you were to cut open this cast iron object you would see that there would be tiny holes everywhere. for a very dense metal object such as a cannonball this does not matter as there's so much iron around it it is not brittle because of how thick it is. however if a person is trying to make a sword which is a nice thin slice of metal to cut someone with d cast iron will show its faults as it will be really brittle because there is only soI saw much surface area in between the holes. A sword or other weapon that is used for slicing or hacking should be able to be withstand repeated abuse and be able to block or Parry a sword or other hacking device that comes to it. if a sword is to brittle it will crack dust be useless so casting a sword it's not a very good long-term solution.

This is why if you go to a traditional Smithy YOU SEE a Smith hammering away at Hot Iron bars. hammered iron is called wrought iron This means that all little bubbles that are forming in iron will be Smashed into each other if you were to cut open a wrought iron piece what a person would find is that it looks like a cheese stick its many many many tiny layers so like carbon fiber it's made out of string that's been pressed together. you can also tell if iron has been wrought and properly cooled is that if the iron is no longer magnetic. in the Bronze Age there is some evidence that weapons were casted however as seen before they are very brittle and since most of the casting of the metal went to the blade to handle had to be riveted and was very weak so often or not any Bronze Age swords broke. another reason why molds are often not used is that the mold itself is very easy to break if it is heated up too quickly as it is Rock so it can stracture exposure. And movies even if they're using a mold they often don't even use a correct Walt as an early example with the Uruk-hai from Lord of the Rings the blades they were making were being poured into open Waltz with only half the mold there. this does not make any sense as only half the iron would be in the shape of a sword while the other half would be a flat. all the bubbling off of the iron also have the exposed side to the air become littered with craters as the iron cools. As you would expect the sword would be useless and so this is why all items that must sustain repeated impacts without breaking are hammered and not cast.

Giant Rats are real

Have you ever seen a giant rat in a video game and talk to yourself that's just your fantasy. well turns out those rats are possible kind of. Discuss the subject one must first learn about cells most importantly haploid and diploid cells that go through meiosis. human now cells that go through meiosis are located in the testes and these cells are called sperm each sperm is a haploid cell with the pathogen is information needed to create life. the other haploid cell that the sperm needs to combine with deform life is the egg inside a human female this egg is also a haploid and has also about half the genetic information needed for life. when two haploids meet they will combine into a diploid zygote this sell Canal divide eventually becoming a human fetus. however if more than one sperm enters the egg that can become a triploid or greater. now the problem with a triploid it's not his not viable for life because the sperm dna cannot make homologous pairs with other cells as there's just not enough this is why only when even amount of haploids combine then they can form homologous pairs. so for a polypoid e animal that has say three sperm enter an egg it will be able to form homologous pairs because there is an even amount of hoploads. Inhumans having a polyploidy fetus will end in stillbirth because humans are unable to support this type of life however it has been recorded and Seed in animals such as rats that when they polyploidy fetus is created that can be born and it is noticed that it will be bigger than most other fetuses. so here's my theory. instead of once sperm entering an egg, how about 5001 enter the egg. the rat that is born probably going to be huge And grotesque looking. However this giant rat will be a rat that is found in our video games a massive rat that's super aggressive it's very strange looking.

The Universe and it's Big Boyos

What is the universe? I'll tell you what, the universe is magical and mysterious. Well, the universe has been debunked. God, what is God; he is the ruler of the universe. Some people say what I say is he is the ruler of our physical world but only our world has a distinction I must make. Before moving on one must realize that there are multiple gods and God is the only god of our world called Earth he controls everything on it that he can see this will be my first illustration of God's gaze. You may feel a pressure on yourself that is about 9.8 meters per second squared down on you. Scientists may say this is gravity however Believers say this is God's gaze. When God looks at something a pressure of his gaze launches itself onto the receiver and the receiver feels this gaze as pressure The scientist quantify this as 9.8 meters per second squared. Principle of God's gaze explains many quandaries about our material world Such as a y space travels so hard because when a rocket releases itself from our atmosphere it will no longer be in the realm of God as it will be and the Eternal Darkness ruled by the void Lords this is a topic for a later section. Another quandary that God's gaze explains quantum mechanics when a scientist tells you that quantum mechanics are hard and very confusing as they make no sense this is because God cannot see the quantum world as they are too small for him to visibly see. This is why some principles of quantum mechanics work the way they do when you look at a particle and quantum mechanics you know you do not know the state of the particle it could either be going left right spinning up or down but because God cannot see this particle he does not decide whether or not it is in a position so scientists have to guess and say it isn't all position. The reason the uncertainty principle is on certain is because God is uncertain and when God isn't certain we are concerned.

Some groups may say there is only one God. And other groups may say But the moon landing was faked both these groups are wrong. The moon landing was indeed true however the science that brought them there was false when an object leaves the sphere of influence about Earth it leaves God's grounds and enters a realm that God the cannot control as he is too small of being compared to other beings have lived in the void for millennia. These beings These beings that live in the void As I Shall Now call the Lords of the dark have Boring over territory was in the dark for Millennia as a search for the quantum points or as I like to call it the new Big Bang. This Quantum Point carries great amount of energy And this energy is what the route through Lords of the dark use as their food you may look at a black hole think that is terrifying however this is the mouth of a lord of the dark. So as a rocket ship leaves God sphere of influence it will no longer have the same physics that was on Earth this is why space travels very hard because scientists must not only account for God's gaze But also the Lords of the darks Domain. The only reason scientists have reached the Moon is because they were able to discover the secrets of voidlord gilgamesh's domain this Venture into his Secrets they are able to understand how his domain interacts with a object using this information we are able to reach the minor Supreme Being called the Moon. Alva contrary to probably popular belief The Moon comes from God as a God was once attacked in the ancient Wars of God has lost It supposed gallbladder and this gallbladder does Orbit of God in the void for a lot of years and because God has lost his gallbladder supposedly this explains the movements of the ocean as the water moves back and forth God's bowels move back and forth this is why when something occurs such as an earthquake within the oc3ean something bad happens on Earth as God is sick and his stomach hurts.

Section II

The creation of the universe understood by many scientists seems to be the big bang however when looking at the truth this a misconception of what really happened. In the twilight of the universe a big bang did occur however it Did not create what we believe such as elements that make up the universe no. the Big Bang created the Supreme Being now this supreme being being very bored created the first void Lords now he's forward Lord's rows over there voice with immense power and ended up creating their own planets their own Sons which would eventually be called galaxies however this group of void Lords around 12 is assumed from the scripture. who jealous of the Supreme Beings power so they decided to rise up and fight the Supreme Being eventually after almost a million years of war where the Galaxy was in a fiery mess. the void Lords prevailed however when they destroyed the Supreme Being exploded and this is why the universe is ever-expanding and won't ever stop probably. The energy from the Supreme Being has permeated the universe has created minor beings such as our own God the void Lords of old throughout the Universe have captured most of the energies and created their own domains scientist like the call these galaxies. Avoid Lord uses a black hole as it Center of command because Of a void Lords Fierce eyes it is able To control most of what season is Galaxy this also explains heliocentricity as the sun looks At its solar system And controls each of its planets however our planet God was able to stop most of the sun's control with a thing called the magnetic field. using this magnetic field God is able to hide the fact that he has beings on his planet that is why he makes space travel also so hard because he doesn't want beings escaping the Earth and warning other Lords & beings who wish to eat . God. so scientists have predicted that the sun will finally gain enough energy to be able to break through the magnetic field and finally see for itself what's on Earth's crust. Killing God in the process.

The NHL Tilts

I would call myself a hockey fan. in my Avid watching of this meticulous and beautiful sport I've noticed something very peculiar. Every time a hockey match starts the home team seems to have an advantage and controls the puck in the opposing side for most of the first period. During the second period the teams switch sides and so does the pace of the game. During the second period the opposing team is now controlling the puck and is able to score goals during this second period. In the third period the teams switch sides again and a very obvious happens the home team now gains an overall position of the puck and pace of the game. After, pondering this quandary for chunk of life I have come to the only solution that can possible explain this phenomenon The ice has been tilted. why why would any other explanation be false well some say that coming out of the locker room a team will have a better strategy but this is false cuz hockey is lucky kinda it's also skill but it's also lucky so coaching and strategy is Is negligible to the Supreme Theory. the only Theory that can explain the strange phenomenon is at the Isis tilted so the reason is so hard for hockey players to stop and have equal possession is because it's hard to ice skate up hill I've done it it's hard. now a person may ask why does the NHL tilt their ice that's unfair you might say no it's not I might say the reason they do this is because hockey is unpredictable and no one really scores unless they have an advantage. Now the stilt is not insignificant tilt is about for my calculations 4 degrees you may say 4 degrees that's a small number and I might say you're right but when you're sprinting up a 4 degree incline and it's icy and you're sliding down the other way it's pretty hard friction is hard. People may ask how do you get a 4 degree tilt in your ice cuz when I fill my ice tubs back at home I have flat ice. the Tilted ice comes from the one and only Zamboni has a weird name so it means it's a weird thing the Zamboni has refrigerator on the bottom that when water molecules are placed on top of each other they're frozen Superfast think of taking a tablecloth off table and leaving the glass on top just got to really fast before I do that over and over again until you have a 4 degree incline on your tire icy surface actually you're very impressive stuff. critics of this theory state that symbol means have only been invented recently so how can the 4 degree tilt be done in the olden days?

I must now speak of the Great Ice Carvers. Back in 1803 what hockey was invented by the In the British Columbia a problem was occurring by 1850 no one could score a goal they tried but they couldn't ice is slippery it's kind of hard to go up and down when all you have is moccasins. Saw an ancient tradition was revitalized and this was ice carving hockey players thoughts of themselves well if I can't move on the ice what if I make Gravity move me on the ice. and so when the first six NHL teams were formed back probably around 1820 I'm going to guess the ice Carvers will show up to every game before the game and then meticulously with the hammer and chisel Carly I said beautiful 4 degree angle. Now that the great goal scoring era don't stop every other. Schools to be scored just amazing however after the

Advent of the ice skate both teams could kind of score even if they were on the tilt.

Made in the USA
San Bernardino, CA
13 June 2020